Our Crumbling Foundation—

Will God Cancel Us?

Mist Carter

LeRue Press, LLC
Lrpnv.com

Our Crumbling Foundation
Copyright ©2021 by Mist Carter

All rights reserved.

Printed in the United States of America by LeRue Press (LRP). No part of this book may be used or reproduced, in any manner whatsoever, performed, or copied in any form without written permission except in the case of brief quotations embodied in critical articles and reviews. For information, contact LeRue Press, 280 Greg Street, Suite 10, Reno, NV 89502. www.Lrpnv.com

ISBN: 978-1-938814-68-6

Updated Edition 2023

DEDICATION

I dedicate this book to my family on earth and in heaven and the friends who encouraged me during this venture. I would also like to thank Jesus for sending that stranger I met on the plane who helped guide me to my salvation. And, finally, this is dedicated to my fellow patriots who love God and love our country enough to do what is necessary to secure our foundation.

TABLE OF CONTENTS

CHAPTER 1
"IN THE BEGINNING…"
Page 1

CHAPTER 2
(To Quote Hillary) "WHAT HAPPENED?"
Page 7

CHAPTER 3
With A Pen and a Mask…
Executuve (Dis)order
Page 13

CHAPTER 4
Does the Congress Really
Represent "We The People"?
Page 27

CHAPTER 5
In Our "Cancel Culture" -
Just Cancel Hypocrisy!
Page 33

Chapter 6
So Now What? How Do
We Restore America?
Page 41

CHAPTER 1
§

"IN THE BEGINNING..."

The first verse in the Bible states: "In the beginning God created the heavens and the earth." (Genesis 1:1 NLT). In addition, the preamble to the Declaration of Independence states the following:

> When in the course of human events, it becomes necessary for one people to dissolve the political bands which have connected them with another, and to assume among the powers of the earth, the separate and equal station to which the laws of nature and of nature's God entitle them, a decent respect to the opinions of mankind requires that they should declare the causes which impel them to the separation.
>
> We hold these truths to be self-evident that all men are created equal; that they are endowed by their Creator with certain unalienable rights; that among these are life, liberty, and the pursuit of happiness; that, to secure these rights, governments are instituted among men, deriving their just powers from the consent of the governed; that whenever any form of government becomes destructive of these ends, it is the right of the people to alter or to abolish it, and to institute new government, laying its foundation on such principles, and organizing its powers in such form, as to them shall seem most

likely to effect their safety and happiness. Prudence, indeed, will dictate that governments long established should not be changed for light and transient causes; and accordingly all experience hath shown that mankind are more disposed to suffer, while evils are sufferable than to right themselves by abolishing the forms to which they are accustomed. But when a long train of abuses and usurpations, pursuing invariably the same object, evinces a design to reduce them under absolute despotism, it is their right, it is their duty, to throw off such government, and to provide new guards for their future security. Such has been the patient sufferance of these colonies; and such is now the necessity which constrains them to alter their former systems of government…

And finally, the Treaty of Paris of 1763 ended the French and Indian War (also called the Seven Years' War) between Great Britain and France, as well as their respective allies. In the terms of the treaty, France relinquished all its territories in mainland North America, effectively stopping any foreign military threat to the British colonies there. This document begins with the following:

In the Name of the Most Holy and Undivided Trinity, Father, Son, and Holy Ghost. So be it.

We must not ignore the significant influence the faith of many Americans, from the Puritans to the present day, had on the founding of our nation. Christian ideas underlie some key tenets of America's constitutional order. The founders believed that humans are created in the image of God, which led them to design institutions and laws meant to protect and promote human dignity. The foundation our Founding Fathers established was clearly biblical and centered around the God of the Bible. They clearly thought moral considerations should determine and influence legislation. They understood that law, justice, and truth are closely related. You cannot do justice without truth. I guess the present-day media missed the memo on that!

They were also committed to liberty, but they never imagined that judges, politicians, and Americans would manipulate provisions of the Bill of Rights. Sadly, America has drifted from these first principles. Relativism has permeated the foundation of America.

History is filled with an abundance of quotes from our Founding Fathers and other key figures during our early years as a new nation. Here are a few of them:

> I verily believe Christianity necessary to the support of civil society. One of the beautiful boasts of our municipal jurisprudence is that Christianity is a part of the Common Law…There never has been a period in which the Common Law did not recognize Christianity as lying its foundations. (Supreme Court Justice Joseph Story, Harvard Speech, 1829)
>
> In my view, the Christian religion is the most important and one of the first things in which all children, under a free government ought to be instructed…No truth is more evident to my mind than that the Christian religion must be the basis of any government intended to secure the rights and privileges of a free people. (Noah Webster, preface, *Noah Webster Dictionary*, 1828)
>
> God who gave us life gave us liberty. Can the liberties of a nation be secure when we have removed a conviction that these liberties are the gift of God? Indeed I tremble for my country when I reflect that God is just, that His justice cannot sleep forever. (Thomas Jefferson, Jefferson Memorial)

> Our laws and our institutions must necessarily be based upon and embody the teachings of the Redeemer of mankind. It is impossible that it should be otherwise; and in this sense and to this extent our civilization and our institutions are emphatically Christian…This is a Christian nation." (United States Supreme Court Decision in *Church of the Holy Trinity v. United States,* 1892)
>
> [The Bible] is the rock on which our Republic rests. (Andrew Jackson)

Individually and collectively as a nation, we must come to the sobering realization and confess that we have turned our backs on God. How long will He patiently put up with the disintegration of our nation's foundation? Has He started to turn His back on us and increasingly remove His hand of protection and blessing? For the past two hundred plus years, sin in the form of power, greed, ego, hatred, and pure evil has slowly, but surely, eaten away at our principles and tenets of our Christian nation. Just take a look back at the last hundred years, or even as recent as the past sixty years.

There are many parallels between Christian theology and political democracy. This is often not the case of most other worldviews, where many religious systems directly conflict with various aspects of democracy. History has shown a reasoned relationship between a culture's religious beliefs and its political stance. The gold standard for freedom and human rights is nations with a Christian heritage. And when forces are in opposition to democracy seek control, one of their first targets is the Christian faith.

Christianity tends to have a dependence on the moral fiber of the culture. Whereas in dictatorships, where a single person's moral compass directs the nation's laws and policies, a democracy goes where the culture goes. That can be good or bad. It becomes bad when a culture drifts away from good moral principles. When that happens, we become defenseless against a shift to abuse of power that will erode freedom.

Benjamin Franklin said, "Man will ultimately be governed by God or by tyrants." I'm convinced that good ole Ben was talking about 2021. When a culture abuses its democratic power, the result is chaos and ruin. When true democracy isn't maintained, it succumbs to a nondemocratic system, usually by force through political schemes and propaganda over time. Modern democracy grew out of a culture steeped in a Judeo-Christian worldview. Yet our nation's culture has slowly moved from that worldview, making us less harmonious in so many ways. When we continually ignore and/or reject God's ways and repeatedly follow paths that are destructive and immoral, we will eventually pay a terrible price. We will pay it as a nation, leading to conflict and social disruption and widespread evil.

America, a nation whose origins believe in God's sovereignty and providential hand, is among the nations who need to heed the Word of God and repent. Look what is printed on our dollar bill: *"In God we trust."* That's quite a strong statement and declaration to make. Our nation was shaped by a belief that the hand of God was somehow involved in its destiny. We used to believe that God was involved in America. Do we still? America's blessings and America's greatness are due to God's blessing and God's faithfulness. God made America the envy of the world, and God will hold America accountable. Has God given up on America? Has He taken his hand off the land? Not yet. But we may be close to that time when He will.

Our way of life; our exceptionalism; our religious freedoms; our system of taxation; our legislative process; our judicial system; and our freedom of speech, freedom to bear arms, will all be threatened and doomed to destruction if the Socialist agenda continues to encroach on our nation like a biblical swarm of locusts. There are only two things that can save America: God and His people. We must be partners with Him in the saving of America.

We can't sit back, throw in the towel, and surrender to evil. God is expecting us to pick up the sword (figuratively, or AOC will post another video) and fight for what is right in His eyes. We can't do it without God, and we can't do it if we're unwilling to fight.

Don't lose hope. God has not abandoned us...
yet! Lean on Him and His Word.

Then when you call, the Lord will answer.
"Yes, I am here," He will quickly reply.
—Isaiah 58:9 NLT

CHAPTER 2

(To Quote Hillary) "What Happened?"

Our nation has been on this Socialist/Marxist course for well over a century, through a drip, drip, drip process similar to gaslighting. Yet most of America has not even been aware of this transition in ideology that has been transpiring. The term *gaslighting* originated from a 1938 stage play by Patrick Hamilton titled *Gas Light* in which an abusive husband attempts to render his wife insane by slowly manipulating small components in their environment while denying these events when his wife raises concern. Over time, the wife is mistaken, confused, or delusional when she notices the changes. The play's title refers to the husband's diabolical acts of slowly dimming the gas lights in the home claiming that his wife's perception of the infringing darkness is evidence of insanity.

Over the years, socialism has ebbed and flowed into the economic, social, and political arenas of many nations, including the United States. The wide array of interpretations and definitions of socialism across the political spectrum and the lack of a common understanding of what socialism is or how it looks in practice reflect its complicated evolution. Nonetheless, socialist parties and ideas continue to influence policy in nations around the world. And socialism's persistence speaks to the enduring appeal of calling for a more egalitarian society.

Socialism is a creeping disease. It is quiet and deadly. It offers much and delivers almost nothing except extensive government ownership and control of the economy. Just prior to the election in 2016, the move to turn up the gas, so to speak, on methods and propaganda to put socialism on stage has escalated. This planned takeover for America is infiltrating every aspect of our society: religion, education, politics, economics, family, morality, etc.

We see a concerted effort in government, in education, in the media, and in virtually every other institution of society to subvert the moral foundations upon which our nation was founded. The basic principles of reverence for God and respect for God's moral laws are under relentless attack by those who reject God and any kind of moral absolute whatsoever.

It should be noted that Karl Marx, who is closely identified with the concept and ideology of socialism, was an atheist. At its core, socialist philosophy is atheistic and antifamily. According to socialist ideology, basic social structures like the church and the family are oppressive and need to be abolished. America was founded on freedom and the right of every individual to pursue their own dreams. Socialism, by contrast, results in everyone experiencing the same nightmare and makes everyone into a slave of the state.

The American Left is the driving force behind socialism in America. Let's be clear: socialism is anti-American. The Founding Fathers did not give us a socialist state; they gave us a representative republic. America is not a democracy, as you may have been taught in school. America is a representative republic.

The first step of ideological subversion is often referred to as brainwashing. This process has been going on for over sixty years, or over three generations, and has not been challenged or counterbalanced. When people are demoralized, they are unable to assess true information. And the past several years have certainly been demoralizing with all the evil, hate, divisiveness, and violence. This has particularly impacted millennials and Gen Z folks because of the breakdown in our education system. Because of the dumbing down of curriculum, the removal of actual and factual history, and instead focusing on gender issues, their minds have been altered and confused. They wouldn't believe facts even if presented with them. To make it worse, these people are and/or will soon be our civic leaders, educators, and parents...Help!

Would these same millennials choose socialism, if in exchange for "free" education and "free" health care, they would have to give up their personal property, such as their iPhone? Would seven percent of millennials declare their willingness to live under communism if they knew the real costs of communism as practiced in some forty nations over the past century—the denial of free speech, a free press, and free assembly; the imprisonment and execution of dissidents; no free and open elections; no independent judiciary or rule of law; and the dictatorship of the Communist Party in all matters and on all occasions? I don't think so!

It's important to remember that as Americans, we all share the same privilege of having been born in the most free society in the world, one which does provide endless potential for upward mobility. Why do you think so many immigrants, legal and illegal, are so desperate to come to America? To sacrifice this freedom in the pursuit of a more rigid economic structure based on an ideology that has, more often than, not failed, would be dangerous. Just look at Venezuela. Do you think when Hugo Chavez became Venezuela's president, he promised that in ten years, people would be hunting rats out of dumpsters to feed their families? Socialism does not work!

Why do so many young people fall victim to the unrealistic and damaging proposals put forth by the radical left? The simplest answer is this: These promises sound good on paper. Upon even the slightest bit of further review, however, they start to fall apart. The truth is hidden from them!

A fifteen-dollar-per-hour minimum wage sounds great, but those who advocate for this are missing a few key points. A minimum wage that high would force businesses, especially smaller and family-owned establishments, into mass layoffs of thousands of entry-level employees. This would be a problem under normal circumstances but would certainly be magnified by the toll of another COVID-19 type of lockdown. Yet, many illegal aliens would benefit, now wouldn't they?

Businesses simply cannot afford to pay entry-level employees that type of money, when their jobs could just as easily be cut or replaced by technology. Several businesses have used the implementation of touchscreen kiosks for in-store ordering, and these kiosks work for free, so to speak. And you don't have to provide health benefits, etc.

We do not always have a grateful heart and take time to thank God for our freedoms—the freedom to worship Him, freedom of choice about our education, freedom to pursue a career, freedom to select a doctor or dentist, freedom to drive a car, freedom to fly the American flag, freedom to vote (despite the voting system being under suspicion), freedom to legally own a gun, etc.

Don't let our government get hijacked. Please, let's not drink the Kool-Aid. If we don't stay firm in our beliefs and prayerfully lean on our Creator, the radical left will get all they want on their wish list, and their wish list should alarm us all. Some of their socialist aspirations include the following: elimination of the Electoral College; sanctuary cities, states, and nation; an education curriculum that includes the 1619 Project, critical race theory, transgender and sexual identity subjects for elementary schools; taxpayer-funded abortion-on-demand until birth to Planned Parenthood; comprehensive LGBTQ agenda (glad there are twenty-six letters in the alphabet); expanding the number of justices on the Supreme Court; higher taxes on middle class and above; complete open borders (even during a pandemic); strict gun control laws that may even amend the Second Amendment; getting back into the Iran Nuclear Deal; radical redistribution of wealth; implementation of the HR 1 bill that will radically impact voting to favor the left; major cuts in our military defense; and finally...everything is racist!

So as the title of this chapter asks, "What Happened?" Part of the answer and responsibility lies with us, Christian patriots. We have either let our guard down, put God on a shelf for a time or two, and decided "We can't beat them, so why vote?" have not spoken up at a city council or board of education meeting; have not written letters to state-, local- and/or federal-elected representatives; haven't peacefully protested (notice I said "peacefully"); or all of the above. First and foremost, we need to get on our knees and ask for courage, wisdom, and guidance from Almighty God.

Keep the faith!

Have mercy on us and help us, if you can. What do you mean, "If I can"? Jesus asked. Anything is possible if a person believes.

—Mark 9:22-23 NLT

CHAPTER 3

—§—

WITH A PEN AND A MASK...
EXECUTUVE (DIS)ORDER

My goodness, I bet he's got a bad case of writer's cramp. In just his fifteen days in office, President Joe Biden has signed a whopping forty-five executive orders (or disorders!). Take a moment to examine and see if this is moving our nation in a forward or backward direction.

Date	Topic	Reversal	Summary
*1/20/21	China Virus	No	Launches a "100 Days Masking Challenge" asking Americans to wear masks for one hundred days and requires masks and physical distancing in federal buildings, on federal lands and by government contractors, and urges states and local governments to do the same
*1/20/21	China Virus	Yes	Stops the United States' withdrawal from the World Health Organization, with Dr. Anthony Fauci becoming the head of the delegation to the WHO
1/20/2021	China Virus	No	Creates the position of COVID-19 Response Coordinator, reporting directly to Biden and managing efforts to produce and distribute vaccines and medical equipment
1/20/2021	Economy	No	Extends the existing nationwide moratorium on evictions and foreclosures until at least March 31

Date	Topic	Reversal	Summary
1/20/2021	Economy	No	Extends the existing pause on student loan payments and interest for Americans with federal student loans until at least September 30
*1/20/21	Environment	Yes	Rejoins the Paris climate accord, a process that will take thirty days
*1/20/21	Environment	Yes	Cancels the Keystone XL Pipeline and directs agencies to review and reverse more than one hundred Trump actions on the environment
*1/20/21	Equity	Yes	Rescinds the Trump administration's 1776 Commission, directs agencies to review their actions to ensure racial equity
*1/20/21	Equity	No	Prevents workplace discrimination on the basis of sexual orientation or gender identity
*1/20/21	Census	Yes	Requires noncitizens to be included in the census and apportionment of congressional representatives
*1/20/21	Immigration	No	Fortifies DACA after Trump's efforts to undo protections for undocumented people brought into the country as children
*1/20/21	Immigration	Yes	Reverses the Trump administration's restrictions on US entry for passport holders from seven Muslim-majority countries
*1/20/21	Immigration	Yes	Undoes Trump's expansion of immigration enforcement within the United States
1/20/2021	Immigration	Yes	Halts construction of the border wall by terminating the national emergency declaration used to fund it
1/20/2021	Immigration	No	Extends deferrals of deportation and work authorizations for Liberians with a safe haven in the United States until June 30, 2022
1/20/2021	Ethics	No	Requires executive branch appointees to sign an ethics pledge barring them from acting in personal interest and requiring them to uphold the independence of the Department of Justice

Our Crumbling Foundation

Date	Topic	Reversal	Summary
1/20/2021	Regulation	Yes	Requires executive branch appointees to sign an ethics pledge barring them from acting in personal interest and requiring them to uphold the independence of the Department of Justice
1/21/2021	China Virus	No	Accelerates manufacturing and delivery of supplies for vaccination, testing and personal protective equipment
1/21/2021	China Virus	No	Directs FEMA to expand reimbursement to states to fully cover the cost for National Guard personnel and emergency supplies
1/21/2021	China Virus	No	Establishes the Pandemic Testing Board to expand US coronavirus testing capacity
1/21/2021	China Virus	No	Establishes a preclinical program to boost development of therapeutics in response to pandemic threats
1/21/2021	China Virus	No	Enhances the nation's collection, production, and sharing and analysis of coronavirus data
1/21/2021	China Virus	No	Directs FEMA to create federally supported community vaccination centers
*1/21/21	China Virus	No	Directs the Department of Education and HHS to provide guidance for safely reopening and operating schools, childcare providers, and institutions of higher education
1/21/2021	China Virus	No	Calls on the Occupational Safety and Health Administration to release clear guidance on Covid-19, decide whether to establish emergency temporary standards, and directs OSHA to enforce worker health and safety requirements
*1/21/21	China Virus	No	Requires mask wearing in airports and on certain modes of transportation, including many trains, airplanes, maritime vessels and intercity buses. International travelers must provide proof of a negative COVID-19 test prior to coming to the US

Date	Topic	Reversal	Summary
1/21/2021	China Virus	No	Creates the COVID-19 Health Equity Task Force to help ensure an equitable pandemic response and recovery
*1/21/21	China Virus	No	A presidential directive to restore America's leadership, support the international pandemic response effort, promote resilience for future threats and advance global health security and the Global Health Security Agenda
*1/22/21	Economy	Yes	Restores collective bargaining power and worker protections for federal workers and lays the foundation for $15 minimum wage
1/22/2021	Economy	No	Calls for assistance to those who are struggling to buy food, missed out on stimulus checks, or unemployed
1/25/2021	Economy	No	Strengthens Buy American rules by closing loopholes and reducing waivers granted on federal purchases of domestic goods
*1/25/21	China Virus	Yes	Reinstates COVID-19 travel restrictions for individuals traveling to the United States from the Schengen Area, the United Kingdom, Ireland and South Africa
*1/25/21	Equity	Yes	Reverses the Trump administration's ban on transgender Americans joining the military
*1/25/21	Equity	No	Directs the Department of Housing and Urban Development to review the Trump administration's regulatory actions for their effects on fair housing and to then "take steps necessary" to comply with the Fair Housing Act
*1/25/21	Equity	No	Directs the attorney general not to renew federal contracts with private prisons
*1/25/21	Equity	No	Recommits federal agencies to "engage in regular, robust and meaningful consultation with Tribal governments"

Our Crumbling Foundation

Date	Topic	Reversal	Summary
*1/25/21	Equity	No	Acknowledges the rise in discrimination against Asian Americans and Pacific Islanders in the past year, directing the Department of Health and Human Services to consider issuing guidance on best practices to improve "cultural competency, language access and sensitivity toward AAPIs" in the federal government's Covid-19 response, and directs the Department of Justice to partner with AAPI communities to prevent hate crimes and harassment
*1/27/21	Environment	No	Elevates climate change as an essential element of US foreign policy and national security and kicks off development of a new emissions reduction target, which will be announced by April 22
*1/27/21	Environment	No	Reestablishes the President's Council of Advisors on Science and Technology
*1/27/21	Environment	No	Charges the director of the Office of Science and Technology Policy with responsibility for ensuring scientific integrity across federal agencies
*1/28/21	Health Care	No	Reopens enrollment on HealthCare.gov from Feb. 15 through May 15, and directs federal agencies to reexamine policies that may reduce or undermine access to the Affordable Care Act
*1/28/21	Health Care	Yes	Rescinds the "Mexico City Policy," a ban on US government funding for foreign nonprofits that perform or promote abortions
*2/2/21	Immigration	Yes	Revokes Trump's order justifying separating families at the border and creates a task force that recommends steps to Biden to reunite separated families

17

Date	Topic	Reversal	Summary
*2/2/21	Immigration	Yes	Aims to address economic and political causes of migration, works with organizations to provide protection to asylum seekers and ensures Central American asylum seekers have legal access to the United States. Rescinds Trump administration policies and guidelines and also initiates a review of policies "that have effectively closed the U.S. border to asylum seekers"
*2/2/21	Immigration	Yes	Rescinds Trump's memo requiring immigrants to repay the government if they receive public benefits. Elevates the role of the executive branch in promoting immigrant integration and inclusion, including reestablishing a task force on new Americans and requires agencies to review immigration regulations and policies

I've highlighted some of the most impactful executive (dis) orders Biden has signed in his very brief tenure as POTUS with an asterisk by the date. You can see that all but one of these highlighted orders are *reversals* of the progress, protection, and prosperity from which our nation benefited as a result of the actions President Trump took while in office. It doesn't take a genius to see that the Biden administration is hell-bent on canceling any victory or success Trump's actions produced. "Come on, man"….is that any way to govern? Vengeance, hatred, and deceptive governance is a disastrous way that any administration should rule. So let's take a closer look at the damaging impact some of these executive (dis) orders will have.

China Virus Executive Orders

The World Health Organization (WHO) is an agency within the United Nations and was formed in 1948. The United States has been its biggest contributor of money to fund its efforts. WHO really came to the limelight when the Chinese virus was publicly introduced to the world in December of 2019 and January of 2020. It is strongly believed that the WHO conspired with China to mislead the US and the world about the nature and origin of the Wuhan virus. As a result, the Trump administration wisely withdrew from that questionable organization in mid 2020.

Former secretary of state Mike Pompeo has been quoted as saying the following: "An epidemic broke out, killing hundreds of thousands of people all across the world. Trillions of dollars lost in economic wealth. All as a direct result of the Chinese Communist Party covering up and doing it with a complicit World Health Organization." During another interview, Pompeo stated this: "That's not an organization that the United States wants to spend roughly half a billion dollars a year supporting. We want to support institutions that are functional and work, and we'll make sure that we do our part to make sure that each of those institutions does just that."

It should also be noted that WHO and other investigators were allowed into China one year after the world was made aware of the virus in order to find out about its origins. Yeah right…how many gallons of disinfectant were poured on every square inch of that Wuhan lab? Interestingly, one of those assigned to this investigative team was a gentleman (I use the term loosely) named Peter Daszak, who is president of EcoHealth Alliance. EcoHealth Alliance is a company that uses taxpayer dollars for its projects, one of which was bat coronavirus research, including virus collection, at the Wuhan Institute of Virology. Ummm…now doesn't that smell fishy or drive you batty?

Bottom line: getting back into the World Health Organization is insane and dangerous. All they want is the big bucks from America, only to allow harm to fall to America and the world. Bad decision, Joe!

Many of the other (dis)orders signed by Biden concerning the China virus are just duplications and plagiaristic actions from what the Trump administration had already adopted and rolled out to the nation. But, Biden ran his campaign on the China virus, so whatever works. Hey Joe, how about signing an executive order demanding that teachers get off their rear ends and return to the classroom to educate our children? Let's see, who's running the country? Is it the Biden administration or the Teacher's Union? Follow the money!

Environment Executive Orders

One of the more egregious executive (dis)orders Biden couldn't wait to sign on day 1 of his administration was cancellation of the Keystone XL Pipeline. Actually, this (dis)order should really fall into the "economy" category instead of the "environment" category. What on earth is this administration thinking? This decision negatively impacts so much, we need to do everything we can to reverse Joe's reversal.

TC Energy Corporation is a Canadian company that owns the Keystone XL Pipeline. Partnering with the United States, this infrastructure project has been several years in the making. Keystone XL is an expansion of an existing pipeline, called Keystone, that carries Canadian crude into the US. The expansion was originally conceived when oil prices were at historic highs—just before the 2008 financial crisis and American shale oil boom—as a vessel that would pump 500,000 barrels of Canadian crude more than 1,700 miles from Alberta to the US Gulf Coast.

The line, which is now partially built but not operating, was eventually expected to transport 830,000 barrels of oil 1,210 miles from the Canadian oil sands to Steele City, Nebraska, where it would link to existing pipelines heading to Gulf Coast refineries. After years of on-again, off-again approvals of the KXL (Keystone XL Pipeline), the Senate approved the bill to build the KXL on January 29, 2015. But wouldn't you know it, Obama vetoed the bill on February 24, 2015. President Trump had campaigned that he would approve the KXL and kept his word by signing an executive order to proceed with this project when he became president.

Sadly, Biden's environmentally obsessed administration believes that canceling the KXL will be a win for the environment, and did so by signing his executive (dis)order reversing Trump's. Not so fast, Joe. Didn't Biden campaign on creating ten million clean energy jobs? Yeah, at what cost?

President Biden's cancellation of the pipeline will not only kill thousands of jobs in both the United States and Canada—something that would provide a postpandemic stimulus necessary to recover the economy from the crisis—but also make America more dependent on oil imports from OPEC+ countries.

Even Russian leaders are dancing in the streets as a result of Biden's "gift" to Russia. Replacement of traditional sources of energy by renewable technologies isn't going to fully be in place overnight, and while the transition is happening, America will have to import more oil and gas from other countries in the interim—just like Germany's dependence on fossil fuels increased following the shutting down of nuclear plants. Wouldn't it be much better for the United States to receive oil from its close ally and neighbor Canada than Saudi Arabia or Russia? Why do you think the Trump administration divorced itself from the Middle East by stopping endless wars that relied on the success of its oil industry? We couldn't have done that without energy independence.

And look at the impact it is having on our relationship with Canada. Do you think Prime Minister Justin Trudeau, who is a climate-change advocate, would have allowed the KXL to go forth if it was detrimental to the environment? The project itself is a contribution to the fight against climate change. This oil from Canada will still be transported through America to the Gulf Coast refineries. But instead of a safer mode of transportation that the pipeline provides, it will move along railways and less carbon-efficient tankers, which is a much more risky means of transportation. In fact, shipping oil by rail or tanker would result in 28 percent to 42 percent higher $CO2$ emissions and be more susceptible to leaks.

But Biden has to satisfy the left-wing mob. So with a mask and a pen, he's signing away GDP revenue, jobs, energy independence, and relationships with our neighbors to the north. Yet, it's a win for Joe and even more so for John Kerry as he skips and prances into the Paris climate accord meetings with a grin from ear to ear, since Joe reversed Trump's order to get out of that useless organization.

Oh, wait a minute, Kerry won't be just skipping. He will be flying in on his private jet that emits upward of forty times more carbon per passenger as commercial jets. According to Kerry when asked why he, as the climate czar, took his private jet to a climate conference in Iceland in 2019, he said, "It was the only choice for somebody like me." Yeah, there's nobody like you, John.

Immigration Executive Orders

I don't know about you, but I'm feeling pretty discouraged right about now because these significant (dis)orders are casting a dark shadow over our next two to four years. Unfortunately, some of these (dis)orders will have lingering effects on our nation even when conservatives are back in the majority leadership. Yet, I'm reminded that God hasn't canceled us, and hopefully He won't. He is in control. Lean on Him and remember His Word: *"God is our refuge and strength, always ready to help in times of trouble."* (Psalm 46:1 NLT)

Let's continue with one more category, immigration, that Biden is dismantling the progress Trump made. Again, nobody is opposed to "legal" immigration which is an important part of growing and succeeding as a nation. But, when laws we already have in place are not followed and/or enforced, and new more destructive (dis)orders are implemented, the crumbling of our nation's foundation is accelerated.

Isn't it amazing how just fifteen years ago, Democrat senators voted for the Secure Fence Act that supported the construction of a physical barrier on our southern border? Those senators included, Hillary Clinton, Barack Obama, cryin' Chuck Schumer, and yes, Joe Biden. But the hatred for Trump was and is so embedded into the minds of the radical left, that they will put US citizens in jeopardy for their safety and economic stability simply to undo everything that Trump did to benefit Americans.

So go ahead, Joe. Allow a substantial number of low-paying entry level positions in certain industries to go to illegal aliens, instead of legal US citizens. Lose tax revenue that can help government programs because employers won't be paying taxes on illegal workers. Burden our hospitals and medical providers with treating illegal aliens for free. Do lower-income US citizens benefit when the terrible schools they're forced to send their children to see class sizes swell with non-English speaking students? The answer is a big fat "No!" And, what about an out-of-control increase in crime, such as drug trafficking, sex trafficking, murder, theft, drunk-driving casualties, and open-door policy for MS-13 gangs? Really? All because you hate Trump? It sounds like you hate your country!

I almost forgot. Aren't we in a pandemic? So how are going to handle the thousands of illegal aliens pouring into our country who may, or may not have the China virus? Let's imagine that we get to give COVID-19 tests to one hundred people a day. And let's say one-third of them test positive. Now what?

Where and how do we quarantine them? Oh my goodness, what if parents who test positive are quarantined and separated from their children during the quarantine period? Congresswoman AOC will come unglued! Remember, Joe, you ran your campaign on ending this pandemic. It's going to be a much bigger task now that borders (the ones you once voted for protecting) are wide open to whoever wants to come in and invade our nation. Unbelievable!

The Biden administration has put an immense focus on making sure that a very large percentage of Americans get a COVID-19 vaccination. Here's the irony. Hundreds of thousands of illegal immigrants have crossed our southern border into the US, a border that the Biden administration claims is closed. Well Joe, it's not closed! It's wide open as a result of the welcome mat you have set in place. There are so many illegals streaming into our country that not all of them can be tested for COVID-19. And the test results of those who have been tested have come back positive. So Joe, why all the emphasis of vaccinating our own citizens when you allow COVID-19 positive illegal immigrants to be released to travel throughout our country? It doesn't make sense!

Okay…the truth! The main reason the radical left is not willing to secure our southern border is because they want and gladly welcome illegal aliens to enter our country and get all situated and comfy. Because come hell or high water, the radical left will find any means (legal or not) to ensure these new invaders of our nation become the voting base for the Dems in the near future. It's all about power! Power at any cost because they really don't care about America.

Most Americans, regardless of political party, are in favor of "legal" immigration. Immigrants who have come to the United States legally have made a great contribution to our nation. And many have gone through the process of becoming legalized citizens. These folks know more about our history and how our government works than most natural-born citizens. But this disastrous and inhumane invasion of "illegal" immigrants since Joe took office, has pulled back the curtain on Mexican drug and human-trafficking cartels and the evil they are exploiting. And what about the thousands of children that are huddled together like sardines in those aluminum blankets, many who have tested positive to COVID-19?

Hey Joe, I thought you ran your campaign on your promise to combat COVID-19. The media and leftists blamed Trump for having "kids in cages" despite the fact that these cages were from the Obama days. But now, the Biden administration doesn't call them cages. They call them "facilities"! Hey Joe, it looks like you and your wonderful VP have your heads buried in one of those aluminum blankets. "Come on, man!"

I say enough is enough! We as Conservatives need to take action now and do everything we possibly can to take back the House and the Senate in 2022, as well as the White House in 2024. By then, so much damage will have already taken place as a result of Biden's (dis)orders that erosion to our nation's foundation will leave many scars.

Stay strong!

When the godly are in authority, the people rejoice.
But when the wicked are in power, they groan.
—Proverbs 29:2 NLT

CHAPTER 4

Does the Congress Really Represent "We the People"?

The economic and psychological impact this pandemic has had on the American people is enormous. So many people have not been allowed to return to their jobs because of very strict restrictions imposed upon small businesses to reduce the spread of the China virus. Initially, in March of 2020, each state laid out their specific guidelines with the purpose of "flattening the curve." Well, the curve did flatten in many states, but the restrictions lingered and often times became even stricter. All the while, big businesses like Walmart, Home Depot, and others were allowed to remain open. When you think about it, Walmart sells tons of products that are manufactured in China, so no wonder the economic impact for that country wasn't as severe as here in America. Could have been the plan all along, since that horrible virus started in a Wuhan lab!

It's sad that so many small businesses, especially restaurants were so heavily impacted. So, the government came to the rescue, so to speak, with the CARES Act in March giving small businesses loans and individuals who qualified $1,200 relief checks. The Congress promised to pass a second relief bill to help Americans and American small businesses. But, not surprisingly, Nancy Pelosi and Chuck Schumer were not willing to work with Republicans *before* the presidential election. Instead, they played their political games and waited until *after* the election to give relief to Americans.

Oh, while some help went to our nation, our wonderful Congress attached a huge $1.4 trillion omnibus bill under the guise of the $900 billion COVID Relief Bill...an omnibus that mainly benefited other nations.

Oh, Nancy, still up to your old tricks of presenting a very lengthy bill (5,593 pages to be exact) at the eleventh hour, which gave little or no time to read the contents before forcing a vote. Wow, that certainly sounds familiar. Can you say *Obama care*? It's sad when our elected representatives cram so much pork into very costly bills without the transparency, debate, and full understanding of the impact such a bill will have, especially when foreign nations are cared for much better than our own citizens.

Here are some examples of the pork that was stuffed into the omnibus bill...hold on to your hat: Not all funding went to foreign nations. The legislation allocated $26,400,000 to the Kennedy Center, $154,000,000 to the National Art Gallery, and $14,000,000 to the Woodrow Wilson Center. Part of these funds will go toward restoration efforts for these facilities; all the while, BLM and antifa groups are tearing down historical statues of heroes of our American history. Oh, and let's not forget that on page 2487 of the bill, the Congress couldn't wait to repeal of criminal penalties for using Smokey Bear's and Woodsy Owl's likenesses without permission. No joke, it's in there!

Foreign nations were the real benefactor of this omnibus bill. As an example, on page 1438, we see that $1,300,000,000 was allocated for foreign Military Financing Program and nation security assistance (including border security) for Iraq, Egypt, Jordan, Lebanon, Saudi Arabia, Morocco, Tunisia, Yemen, Cameroon, Central African Republic, Democratic Republic of the Congo, Chad, Malawi, South Sudan, Cambodia, Laos, Hong Kong, Tibet, Vietnam, Afghanistan, Bangladesh, Pakistan, Sri Lanka, Belize, Costa Rica, El Salvador, Guatemala, Honduras, Nicaragua, Panama, Columbia, Venezuela, etc.

Now wait a minute, why care so much about the border security for foreign nations when you want to stop construction on our southern border? The radical left thinks our borders aren't important, especially when they freely allow potential future Democrat voters into our country. But, if you don't like borders for our nation, how come a huge, expensive border was erected around the capital in January? Oh, it's just Nancy being Nancy!

And we must not forget to allocate funds to "gender programs in Pakistan" to the tune of no less than $10,000,000. And an omnibus bill would not be complete without including efforts to legislate the "Tibetan reincarnation process" of the Dalai Lama, which can be found on page 5100 of the bill. You just can't make this stuff up…it's for real.

Now that we are in 2021 and Biden is in office, the House and Senate have used a tool called budget reconciliation, which allows the Congress to pass Biden's new $1.9 American Rescue Plan Bill, without Republican votes. Along with ridiculous pork added to the COVID-19 relief the bill will provide, the rules have been relaxed on who is eligible to receive such relief.

In the CARES Act from March, households with a person who wasn't a US citizen were not eligible to receive a stimulus check, even if one spouse and a child were US citizens. The federal government categorizes families whose members have different citizenship and immigration classifications as "mixed status." But Biden's plan will now expand eligibility to adult dependents who have been left out of previous rounds of relief and all mixed status households.

As this book is being published, Congress (well it was only the Democrats) passed another stimulus package on March 11, 2021—a $1.9 trillion American Rescue Plan. Of course, like the previous spending packages passed, only a small percentage of this outrageous spending actually goes toward COVID-19 relief. The rest is allocated for the ridiculous pet projects of the left-wing mob, not to mention the extra $600 unemployment benefits being paid.

Where is the logic in paying people more to stay home instead of getting off the couch and returning to the workforce where thousands of job openings exist? This nonsense ultimately forces more small businesses to close and increased prices for goods and services that we all incur. But that's not all. The Biden administration is pushing for a new $2.3 trillion infrastructure plan. Well, you guessed it. If passed, not all of those planned dollars will go toward real infrastructure. Every spending bill by the radical left has to have a big portion go toward climate change.

And who's going to pay for this? The corporate tax rate is proposed to go from 21 percent to 28 percent. And don't be fooled. Individual taxes will increase. Biden's spending imprudence will crush the economy, produce lower revenues, decrease the number of full-time jobs, and lead to run-away inflation. Nice plans, Joe!

The essence of our republic is founded in our faith in God, and a government that operates for "We the People." America certainly wasn't perfect after our Founding Fathers established the government. In fact, America had to go through many brutal growing pains in order to change, adapt, and improve. In our founding, we the people did not really include all of the people. It took a civil war and the loss of approximately 1.5 million lives to finally end slavery in America and include all the people. As a nation, we sinned, confessed, and repented. We're reminded of the scripture verse, "Now repent of your sins and turn to God, so that your sins may be wiped away." (Acts 3:19 NLT).

But in the last several years, our nation has slipped into pretty ugly times. While both Republicans and Democrats have contributed to this crisis, it appears the Democrat party has changed more dramatically. The bitterness we are seeing is coming from a party that has lost its way morally and become increasingly radical, creating this environment of divisiveness.

The Democrats no longer are the party of FDR, Kennedy, Carter, or Humphrey. They are a party led to do anything to destroy a duly elected president and alter or undo key amendments of our Constitution. In their zeal, they have broken laws, attempted two misguided impeachments, tried to cancel many aspects of our culture, and enlisted our national media to achieve these destructive goals.

They want to stack the Supreme Court, that will eventually make a one-party nation that does not represent "We the people." They want to defund the police, yet they sure wanted the police on January 6, 2021. They turn a blind eye to radical groups like BLM and antifa and fail to hold them accountable for their terrorist-like events that have caused death and billions of dollars of destruction to cities across the country. They want to enact a Green New Deal that will result in the loss of jobs and add to the already out-of-control deficit our nation has accrued. They have conspired with our national media. Fake news media and big tech are telling people what to print and view, forcing many to seek the truth through other means. When an opposing view arises, they create censorship in our social media, as well as engage in a phenomenon called *canceling*, which adds to the hatred and divisiveness. Socialism is the final step in the movement from trusting God to trusting the government, a government that no longer supports "We the People."

Don't be fooled!

They promise freedom, but they themselves are slaves of sin and corruption. For you are a slave to whatever controls you.
—2 Peter 2:19 NLT

CHAPTER 5

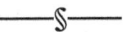

In Our "Cancel Culture" - Just Cancel Hypocrisy!

We are being swallowed by the sink-hole (or stinkhole) that is "cancel culture". Even corporate America is not immune to this poisonous pill, not so much that they support justice, but more so that they are trying to avoid becoming a victim of canceling. As a result, our society is transforming into a dystopia, which by definition is a made-up or imagined place where everything is intolerable—the opposite of utopia. The practice of canceling came into being in the last few years through the expanded power of social media. Millions of posts, tweets, videos, blogs, etc. travel through the algorithms of social media platforms each day. Many of these elicit an emotion of outrage or scandal, because the tech machine exposes these communications to larger audiences than the author of the communication may have intended. A person or group that supports something that others find offensive now becomes the victim of the criticism that grows so rampant that the individual or company is shamed or canceled.

But let's not fool ourselves. The blame does not solely lie with big tech. Big media is in bed with big tech and pulling every string they can to control free speech and real truth. They have joined forces with the radical left. It is alarming and should be one of the most concerning issues of the present time, how much power big tech and big media wield. Through their daily abusive actions disguising or manipulating important news items, the truth is withheld to the citizens (such as all the issues, investigations, and actions of Hunter Biden). Both truth and mistruth influence each of us on how we view various issues and the decisions we make, such as how we vote in an election. This is dangerous to our nation and our freedoms. The motive of controlling information is to control those who receive that information. Media and big tech have too much power, period!

The truth, or lack thereof, has put our country in a constant state of uncertainty, stress, discord, and increased mistrust of the Congress. Look at the wasted time and money spent for the past four plus years to erase Trump from office and history itself through the Mueller probe and two impeachments. My goodness! Our do-nothing Congress is so distracted by these futile efforts that the business of representing the people is certainly not top of mind. The average number of days members of the Congress work per year is shameful. On average, the House of Representatives works 146 days and the Senate, 165. Wouldn't we all like to work so little for a good salary and lifetime pension and health benefits? Throw in these unnecessary distractions like impeachments, and there's no time for anything else. We need term limits!

In place of having truth in our government and media, we have so much hypocrisy that it's not worth our time listing those endless examples. However, the most recent cases of hypocrisy have led to the second impeachment of (former) President Trump. The breach of the US Capitol building on January 6, 2021, was a tragic and inexcusable event that no American or politician (except those who actually caused destruction and harm) condones.

By the way, persons arrested from the January 6 event are still in jail without bail while BLM and antifa looters and arsonists who are destroying cities across our nation get released without bail within hours of the millions of dollars of destruction they have caused. Hypocrisy? Yes!

Yet, the radical left members of the Congress are hell-bent on putting all the blame on Donald Trump. They claim he is to blame as a result of his repeated claims that the 2020 presidential election was full of fraud and malfeasance. They also claim that Trump's last speech at the rally held on January 6 riled the crowd to a frenzy, causing them to storm the Capitol building to cause harm to individuals and to do massive destruction.

Here comes the hypocrisy. Since the tragic death of George Floyd in the summer of 2020, radical left groups like BLM and antifa took the ball and ran (with the generous funding from George Soros) and began to engage in violent acts of vandalism, arson, and looting of several cities across America. Additionally, lives were lost in these nonpeaceful riots. These thugs even attacked local police stations and federal buildings.

But according to the fake news media outlets, these were *peaceful* protests…nothing to see here! The radical left-wing politicians only want to focus on the events at the Capitol on January 6, which again were staged, planned, and funded by haters of America like George Soros. The left has turned a blind eye to the livelihoods lost and the destruction to so many American cities for the past nine months.

The left can claim it was Trump's speech that directed people to invade the Capitol, all the while ignoring the hateful threats spewing from the mouths of our congressmen/women and senators like Maxine Waters, Chuck Schumer, and, yes, even our current vice president, Kamala Harris. Regarding Trump's claims that the election was stolen, didn't Hillary Clinton say on May 15, 2019, "You can run the best campaign, you can even become the nominee, and you can have the election stolen from you"? Oh, and didn't Stacey Abrams challenge her gubernatorial election results in 2018, refuse to concede, and claim the election was unfair? The hypocrisy is out of control. However, our First Amendment gives us the right to freedom of speech. We just shouldn't judge others for what they do or say when we do or say the same thing.

Let's expose a little truth. The left claims that conservatives have tunnel vision and only watch news shows like Fox News, Newmax, or One American News. They claim we only get the conservative point of view. The truth is that these news channels actually have representation from both sides of the political aisle, whereas the left-wing news channels downplay, hide, or twist the context of situations like the border crisis, just to fit their narrative. What if Fox News only showed the arrest and death of George Floyd only one time and since had only one report on the trial of the police officer, Derek Chauvin? This would be using the same modus operandi of mainstream media.

Actually, this is totally opposite of the exposure that the George Floyd tragedy has been given. Fox News has extensively covered this and all other news items. They expose the truth, warts and all. In contrast, remember how little coverage, if any, the fake news media gave to the Hunter Biden laptop issue? The same head-in-the-sand behavior was evident when the mainstream media outlets gave little or no airtime to the report that Hunter Biden may have committed a felony by lying on a background check before purchasing a gun. Oh, that was the same gun that the widow of Hunter's brother, Beau, tossed into a dumpster behind a grocery store in Delaware.

This is in extreme contrast to how fake news media hides the truth to its viewers. I've seen it firsthand. In recent conversations with my Democrat friends (yes, I have Democrat friends), they were not aware that we have a crisis at our southern border. They had not *heard* or *seen* on the news that thousands and thousands of illegal immigrants were pouring into our nation. That's pretty sad!

So let's just expose the hypocrisy of BLM. They are known as an antiracist group. Truth be told, they're not. The term *racism* or *racist* is being carelessly thrown about to label individuals, groups, or events too often on duplicitous grounds. The dictionary defines *racism* as "prejudice, discrimination, or antagonism directed against someone of a different race based on the belief that one's own race is superior." Let's be very clear: racism, true racism is abhorrent. How horrible it must be to live your life believing that anyone who disagrees with you in the slightest is evil and racist.

Slavery has been part of human life since biblical times. Back then, however, it wasn't based on skin color. And, yes, it is true that in the early years of our nation, slavery was part of American culture. It was a grim part of our history. All nations and culture have history, much of which is grim. The question is, do we see and confess the grimness, learn from our mistakes, and change our ways?

Thankfully, Abraham Lincoln (a Republican) began the process to end slavery in America and extend freedom to those enslaved through his Emancipation Proclamation in 1862. Since then, has America been absent of discrimination, prejudice, and racism? Sadly, no! We are all flawed individuals born with a sinful nature. We all have our biases, opinions, and likes/dislikes about things. But that doesn't mean that our biases and opinions are extreme. It is highly likely that the majority of Americans regard the messages of Dr. Martin Luther King very highly, and want see the world as he did, through a color-blind lens. Yet it seems that the radical left has concealed King's message of tolerance, love, healing, and respect and exchanged it for a viewpoint that we *are* our race! We are more than our race, and it is high time we refuse to accept that everything is racist.

Here's another example of hypocrisy the left has demonstrated which involves police involved shooting deaths. A recent example resulted in the death of a young black male, Daunte Wright, during a traffic stop. Officers determined that Wright had an outstanding warrant for aggravated armed robbery. As the officers were attempting to take Wright into custody, he resisted arrest. Tragically, a twenty-six-year female veteran of the Brooklyn Center Police Department, Kim Potter, negligently mistook her service weapon for her taser, and fatally shot Wright, after she had repeatedly warned Wright of her intent by shouting "Taser! Taser! Taser!"

Officer Potter, as well as the Police Chief, resigned within two days following this tragedy. Additionally, Potter was charged with manslaughter the day after her resignation. The media not only identified Potter, they "doxed" her by publishing personal information about her, such as her home address, putting Potter and her family in possible danger.

Let's compare this fatal shooting incident by a law enforcement officer with the tragic event that took place during the US Capitol protest on January 6, 2021. Ashli Babbitt, a thirty-five-year-old Air Force veteran, was fatally shot by an unidentified US Capitol Police Officer when she and others attempted to break into the Speaker's lobby. Video footage of this tragic event shows a plain-clothed African American officer holding his service arm after firing the fatal shot.

Now, here is where the double standard comes into play. Were both victims breaking the law? Yes. But remember, only one had an open warrant for his arrest from an aggravated robbery attempt. And only one resisted arrest and was given a warning that a shot was going to be fired from a taser but, tragically and negligently was from a service weapon. It could be said that the officer that killed the unarmed Babbit was also negligent because he intentionally fired his shot into a mob of people and other officers without verbal warning, which likely would not be audible due to the crowd noise. After an investigation, the DOJ determined that not only would the Capitol Police Officer not face any charges, he would not be identified. Potter on the other hand, was criminally charged and identified immediately for her accidental killing of Wright.

Shooting deaths are all tragic regardless of the race of the victim and or shooter. Here are some statistics to chew on from the Washington Post and reported by Statista.com:

Our Crumbling Foundation

1. In 2020 the total number of people killed by police was 1000
2. Of those, 962 were male and thirty-eight were female
3. 432 were white, 226 were black, 156 were Hispanic, 164 were unknown, and twenty-two were other
4. 622 were armed with a gun, 166 with a knife, fifty-six unknown, forty-seven vehicle, forty-three other weapons, forty-one were unarmed, and twenty-five had a toy weapon.
5. According to the Officer Down website, in 2020 a total of 360 line-of-duty police officers were killed. Of those, forty-five were by gun, fifteen by vehicle assault. So far in 2021, fifteen officers have been killed by gun, two by knife, seven by vehicle assault.

Here's another sad truth. More shooting deaths occur in big cities like Chicago, Detroit, Baltimore, Los Angeles, and New York City as a result on blacks killing other blacks. The rampant gang activity, single-parent homes, poor quality of education, and economic factors result in increased criminal activity. But, does the left-wing media focus on these facts? No. Instead, they promote protests that too often lead to more violence and destruction, blame the police, and do nothing to fix the problems in those democrat-run cities. Just think about the courage it takes for one to pursue a career in law enforcement and put their life on the line every day to protect all citizens, regardless of race. A final truth about police-involved shootings, if people who are stopped by police would simply follow the instructions officers give and stop resisting arrest, then there would be no need for a single shot to be fired!

This is just more evidence how far our nation has drifted from God. Our Creator said, "Then God said, 'Let Us make human beings in Our image and likeness…'" (Genesis 1:26 NCV). God didn't say "Let us make white human beings, or black human beings, or brown human beings" in His image. Furthermore, here are more Scripture verses that address racism:

Peter began to speak: "I really understand now that to God every person is the same. (Acts 10:34 NCV)

Stop judging by the way things look, but judge by what is really right. (John 7:24 NCV)

But if you treat one person as being more important than another, you are sinning. You are guilty of breaking God's law. (James 2:9 NCV)

Be kind and loving to each other, and forgive each other just as God forgave you in Christ. (Ephesians 4:32 NCV)

Bottom line — cancel hypocrisy!

You hypocrite, first take the log out of your own eye, and then you will see clearly to take the speck out of your brother's eye.
—Matthew 7:5 (NASB95)

Chapter 6

So Now What? How Do We Restore America?

The previous chapters have addressed some but not all of the major challenges America faces today. We have spent little time, if any, on abortion, taxes, defunding the police, national security, the opioid crisis, our failing education system, terrorism, trade, deficit spending, or corruption in general. Let's face it, if we took a deep dive into each of these now, we would all need therapy immediately!

Our country is in real serious trouble. The radical left wants to erase any and all progress the Trump administration has made in the last four years. We get it, many conservatives weren't in favor of Trump's tweets, or of all the things of which he spoke, but we were extremely in favor of the advancements through executive order and policy changes that his administration made to make America great again. Each day, the Biden administration is tearing away at the fabric of America's independence, security, morality, freedom, and religious strength. Our borders mean nothing. Our children's education means nothing. Life of the unborn means nothing. Our oil independence means nothing. And success of small business means nothing. More importantly, truth means nothing—truth about COVID-19, truth about corruption, truth about BLM and antifa, truth about illegal immigration, truth about the real crisis at our open border, truth about religious freedom, truth about free speech, truth about our Second Amendment, truth about the Confucius Institute, truth about Planned Parenthood, truth about dirty money funding dirty things, truth about censorship from social media, and the truth about fake-news media.

Here's another truth. The thing that politicians fear the most is the fear of not getting reelected. They have been elected to represent *we the people*. If we the people just sit back and let our elected officials at all levels of government, and regardless of their party, rule without hearing the truth about how their decisions are affecting *we the people*, then we are at fault. It is vital that we communicate with our elected officials to provide feedback on their job performance. If we don't, our elected officials will continue to destroy the fabric and foundation of our nation. If they get a strong sense that their job performance will likely not get them reelected, it could very well change some hearts and minds of those in office. It is certainly worth our effort to speak up.

The hope is that the issues that have been addressed here will give you food for thought and inspire you to do something about it. But we can't do it alone. Now you didn't think having a book title that contained the word *God* would leave Him out of the conversation. In fact, He is the key element in the solution to the state of our nation. There are important actions that must be taken to again build up the foundation of our nation. These will be difficult to hear and challenging to employ.

> Let's start with a couple of godly truths from the Bible:
> Everyone must submit to governing authorities. For all authority comes from God, and those in positions of authority have been placed there by God. (Romans 13:1 NLT)
> For the Lord's sake, yield to the people who have authority in this world: the king, who is the highest authority, and the leaders who are sent by him to punish those who do wrong and to praise those who do right. (Peter 2:13-14 NCV)

In our current situation, these scripture verses are a couple of tough pills to swallow. Our initial response might be, "Really? You can't be serious." It makes us start to question God's motives and purposes. Yet God made it really clear when He told us through His prophet Isaiah, "'My thoughts are nothing like your thoughts,' says the Lord. 'And my ways are far beyond anything you could imagine. For just as the heavens are higher than the earth, so my ways are higher than your ways and My thoughts higher than your thoughts.'" (Isaiah 55:8-9 NLT)

God's ways are higher than our ways because His ways are always part of a bigger plan. He is the Creator and Sustainer of all things. His sovereignty is infinite, and His characteristics of truthfulness, goodness, faithfulness, righteousness, and love are immutable. We view life through our earthly lenses, while God knows and sees all things (past, present, and future) through His divine heavenly perspective.

The world can be a frightening place, yet God is always in control. We just need to believe and trust that His ways are for our ultimate good. We can't always understand why God allows certain people into positions of authority. The Bible cites several incidents when evil leaders ruled. Take, for example, how God ultimately prevailed when Pharaoh, the evil ruler of Egypt, tried to keep the Israelites in slavery. We must recognize the fact that just because something occurs under the providence of God does not mean He condones actions of evil, or that He desires them to occur.

In His providence, God reigns over all human matters. The most prominent example is the crucifixion of Jesus, who was crucified under the authority that God granted to Pontius Pilate. This most evil deed was ordained by God before the world was created. Did Jesus prevail? Yes, and those of us who believe in Him are beneficiaries of that event.

When a nation advocates evil and hatred, God will eventually withhold His blessings slowly but surely. His hope is that we will see the error of our ways, confess those wrongdoings, and correct our behavior. If change does not occur, the ruin and crumbling of that nation is certain. Is it too late? Are we doomed? Well, that depends. We might be thinking to ourselves, *I'm only one person, how can I make any impact?* Or, some might be thinking this: *If I submit to authority that I don't support, doesn't that mean they win?* These are good questions.

So that brings us to our present challenge to "yield" to the current Biden administration who are now in authority. After all we have covered thus far, which reveals the corruption, abuse of power, evil, and disdain for our country, it is extremely difficult to truly trust God by submitting or yielding to our current elected leaders. But that is exactly what we must do, and it starts with totally trusting in God, our solid Foundation.

There are a number of things that "We the People" who love God and love our country can do. Some of these are no brainers, and others might be the most difficult thing we can do. So here we go!

1. Pray, Pray, Pray

Remember the saying, "When the going gets tough, the tough get going"? Well, we need to change it up a bit to say, "When the going gets tough, the tough get on their knees — and pray!" As Christians, we are commanded to pray for our leaders and pray that God will intervene to change the hearts of ungodly leaders. The Apostle Paul wrote in one of his letters,

> Pray for rulers and for all who have authority so that we can have quiet and peaceful lives full of worship and respect for God. (1 Timothy 2:2 NCV).

2. Read the Bible

The Bible gives us the criterion by which we can distinguish truth from error. It tells us what God is like. It is God's Word. The Bible is timeless and truthful and reveals that God does not change and neither does man's sinful nature. There are so many examples in the Bible from which we can learn some invaluable lessons of life, through the experiences of those who came before us. It's a wonderful book of hope — something we can all use about now.

3. Read the Constitution

By reading the Constitution, we can better understand the foundations of our nation and understand the reason for which we fight to preserve it. It's highly likely that our founders expected us to read it so that we could remain a free nation.

4. Vote

Our opinion means nothing if we fail to exercise our right to vote. Voting should not be limited to national elections. It is just as important to vote in local and state elections. (There might be less corruption at those levels, but you never know.) Become informed and educated about what is going on in your community, your schools, your state, and at the federal level. When elections are not corrupt, your vote does count. 2022 just may be the start of truly taking back our nation at all levels.

5. Volunteer for a Political Campaign

If you want to make a positive impact to ensure the right leaders are elected into office, volunteer in a campaign for local, state, or congressional or presidential candidates that will uphold our Constitution and keep us as "One Nation Under God."

6. Attend School Board Meetings

Whether you have school-age children or not, it is vital to be involved in what is actually going on in our schools these days. Challenge those school boards that are exposing your children to material that is objectionable, like gender studies in elementary school. The Teacher's Union has way too much power and is wrongly educating the young minds of our children. Get involved!

7\. Contact Your Elected Officials

Regardless of the political party your elected representative belongs to, they need to hear your concerns and/or praises when the need arises. We may think they don't care what you think, and that could often be the case. But if enough people contact them about issues of concern, it might just influence a change for the better (especially if they are up for reelection!)

8\. Go to Church

Church is a place where you can truly worship God, because He deserves our worship. It's a great place to connect and network with other believers, who more likely than not, share your political views. Secondly, if you have children, youth groups in churches are an amazing arena where your children can mature into responsible, God-loving citizens.

9\. Be Charitable

Donate money to organizations that help the disadvantaged, donate to a church, donate to organizations that help veterans or the disabled, or donate to political candidates that can uphold the tenets of our nation. Volunteer in your community to help those who are less fortunate than you. Spread some goodness around as a counter measure to the evil that is so prevalent. There are numerous organizations that provide amazing assistance to people. For example, we support Samaritan's Purse as they work to meet the needs of people around the world. Here is a link to their website: https://www.samaritanspurse.org

10\. Forgiveness

Gulp! Here's the biggie. Forgiveness is the most difficult thing that God commands us to do. At all levels, no matter the offense, betrayal, rift, or sin that has been committed, without forgiveness, the issue will always remain.

Our Crumbling Foundation

Does it mean that when we forgive someone that we have to like them, forget about what took place, or remain in whatever relationship with them? Absolutely not. Forgiveness does not erase the past, but it does give you a healthier path going forward. Without forgiveness, we allow hatred, anger, and hurt consume us. The person or party that has done you wrong often times doesn't even know how much you are suffering as a result of their actions. So as they go on with their merry life, you remain stuck in your anger, hatred, and hurt. Forgiving others is very freeing for you. Forgiving others is more beneficial to you than you can imagine.

As previously mentioned, we are all full of sin. As Christians, we know that if we confess those sins to God, He will forgive us—every time! Let's not beat around the bush here. Why on earth do you think that Jesus left heaven, came to earth to experience all human emotions, remained sinless, and was gruesomely crucified on a tree that He had created? Why? Because He loves us and wants to forgive us. In those brutal moments, He took on and absorbed each and every one of all the sins ever committed and will be committed from every single human being. Let that sink in for a moment. As that was happening, He said to His Heavenly Father, "Father, forgive them, for they don't know what they are doing." (Luke 23:34 NLT)

So what does this all have to do with the crumbling foundation of our nation? Well, we need to first ask God to forgive us for allowing this to happen. Next, we need to pray for those who willingly and actively took actions (or failed to take actions) that have resulted in the crumbling of our foundation. Not only pray for them, but also *forgive* them for the present and future impact their actions have had on our life and our nation. Again, forgiveness does not mean agreeing with or forgetting about what has taken place, but it can free us to do our part to right the wrong!

We need to take God off the shelf and put Him in the center of our lives and obediently follow the loving guidance and direction He has for us. We need to renew our faith in God. We must remain engaged in this spiritual conflict for the heart and soul of our nation. There's a saying (author unknown), "If you permit it, you promote it!" We must make every effort to stop permitting evil to run in our nation. Do this and God will never cancel us!

For words of comfort and hope from our Creator, I encourage you to read Psalm 37.

Lean on Him!

Trust in the Lord with all your heart and do not lean on your own understanding. In all your ways acknowledge
Him, and He will make your paths straight.
—Proverbs 3:5-6 (NASB95)

ABOUT THE AUTHOR

Mist Carter is a retired corporate manager who became a Christian patriot following retirement. In fact, she gave her life to Christ thirty thousand feet above ground in an airplane, perhaps so she could be closer to heaven from the get-go. God quickly gifted her with a talent to write and lead women's Bible studies. She found that the frequent discussions with friends and family about politics and the state of our nation were not really doing anything to improve the situation. So she decided to write a book of truth hope, and action. She loves God, her country, family, friends, and golf.